WHO STOLE
MY SALE?

WHO STOLE MY SALE?

23 Ways
To Close The Deal

TODD DUNCAN

NELSON BUSINESS
A Division of Thomas Nelson Publishers
Since 1798

TABLE OF CONTENTS

. . .

CLEANING UP THE CHICKEN MEAT

. . .

Sheryl and I arrived at a new San Diego restaurant on opening night. We were seated promptly and served our drinks. Next came our appetizers and a promise that our entrées would be out shortly. Twenty minutes passed, then thirty. We'd waited for good food before so we weren't grumbling yet. Besides, the waiter had kept us informed and our glasses full. We chatted five minutes more and our entrées arrived. It was the rotisserie chicken for me and the mixed grill for Sheryl. The sight and aroma were delightful and well worth the wait.

Then I cut anxiously into my chicken and it exploded. Meaty fragments of white and brown shrapnel littered my shirt and tie. To accelerate its preparation the cook stuck the bird in a pressure cooker which trapped juices between the skin and breast meat. My upper half still paralyzed, I swiveled my head to find Sheryl sawing through her steak like a lumberjack. Apparently it tanned under a lamp while my chicken bomb was being inflated.

When you're in this situation there are two things you can do. You can demand attention and then detail the specifics of what you deserve, or you can trust your waiter's ability to repair the damage.

We opted for the latter and were surprised. The server softly apologized and did nothing more. Then when it was time to leave, he handed us the full bill. In short, he gave us no incentive to return. A sucker for happy endings, I sent the restaurant's owner a letter detailing the debacle and suggesting a better course of action. A little aggressive, I know—but it's the bane of a sales trainer's existence. First, confess your error and then correct the problem immediately, I explained. Finally, communicate to your patrons that you would like another chance to earn their business by offering them an incentive to return.

Shortly thereafter I received a letter from the owner. He took full responsibility, credited my card for the amount of the meal, offered to pay for my dry cleaning, and included a gift certificate for four without monetary limit.

Our return experience was wonderful; and we've confidently

dined there many times since. In fact, it has become a down-town favorite of ours—proof that the debris from one debacle doesn't have to ruin a relationship.

LESSON SUMMARY

The fact that every salesperson makes mistakes is indisputable. To aim for perfection is to invite frustration. Furthermore, it chips away at your authenticity. To be an effective salesperson is to be a person, with a keen knack for helping people meet their needs. The San Diego restaurant owner knew this; his waiter did not. Fortunately for the owner, I gave him a second chance by telling him of his waiter's error, and he took that second chance to make up for a poor first impression.

When you blow it with a customer, don't run from them. Run to them!

Here are actions you must take to recover
a high-trust client whom you've poorly served:

Confess.

Tell the client you blew it and apologize.

No finger-pointing.

Correct.

Tell the client what you are

going to do about it.

Communicate.

Let the client know you value him

and that you want another chance,

and give him an incentive to try you again.

■ ■ ■

HIGH TRUST SELLING

To continually move from your
foundation toward success,

you must have more than perseverance—

you must have the right perception of failure.

■ ■ ■

HIGH TRUST SELLING

Mistakes should never leave you uninspired to continue.
In fact, with the right perception of failure,
you just might be more motivated to sell
after a mistake. That's because a mistake
should not be perceived as a step backward,
but rather a pause for redirection,
an opportunity to make a positive change.

■ ■ ■

HIGH TRUST SELLING

SELLING INK
OR INSPIRATION

· · ·

When the *Los Angeles Times* phoned, Brent was in the mood to do some research. How would a newspaper salesperson handle the truth? The young man calling wasted little time. "Can I tell you a little about our paper?" he asked and then without waiting for an answer he reeled off reasons the *Times* was the right fit. It was one of nation's most respected papers, he insisted. Millions read it daily. It reported the events a west coaster was curious about. And best of all it was cheap if you ordered right away—only pocket-change a day.

When the salesman finally took a breath, Brent chimed in with the truth: he was allergic to newsprint. "That's a new one," the young man choked out between chuckles. "C'mon, you can't be serious."

"I'm completely serious," Brent replied, incredulous. "And you have a nice day." With that he hung up the phone.

A year later the doorbell rang and it was a different story. This time it was a university student selling subscriptions to the local paper. "Whatta ya got?" Brent asked. The young man was knocking on doors, he explained, because each paper he sold helped him pay his tuition. Now Brent's wife was listening. "What are you studying?" she asked.

"I'm premed," he answered, "and I'd like to be a pediatrician one day."

"I was premed for three years," Brent replied as he led the three into the living room.

Standing around the couch and coffee table the three discussed majors and where college might lead a person after he graduates. For ten minutes they chatted, not once mentioning the paper.

Later, when the student walked down the front porch steps and out the driveway, he had a check in his hand and success in his step. Brent and his wife ordered a subscription despite his allergies because they weren't buying ink; they were helping a young man fulfill a dream. There's a big difference.

LESSON SUMMARY

If you're not inspired to sell then how do you expect to inspire others to buy? The *Los Angeles Times* salesman wasn't enthusiastic about his job—he just feared missing his quota. The student, on the other hand, was inspired to sell papers because they were providing for his future hopes and dreams. It makes a difference in you and your customer when you know why you're selling.

For you to build loyal,
lasting relationships with your clients, you must
take the time to know them, not just know about
them. And you must allow them to know you.

■ ■ ■

HIGH TRUST SELLING

Lasting success is built with the
stuff on the inside—

who you are and who you want to become,

why you sell and what legacy you intend to leave.

■ ■ ■

HIGH TRUST SELLING

Selling is what you do in the process of living.

It's not the other way around.

Life does not happen after work is done.

Living is supposed to be supported and

supplemented by selling. Therefore,

you must adapt your selling endeavors to

your most treasured life.

■ ■ ■

KILLING THE SALE

A SERVANT'S
HEART

· · ·

When I met Mona I was in a hurry. Sheryl and
I were leaving the country in less than twenty-four hours
and I needed a couple pairs of pants for the trip. Mona
approached us to help and quickly had me in two pairs of
good looking pants. There was only one problem. The hems
were unfinished and it was Sunday.

Mona insisted it wasn't a problem and excused herself to
phone the tailor. She returned shortly with a promise that
the pants would be ready by five o'clock that evening. I was
delighted. Then she went overboard.

"You're probably going to be very busy packing for your
trip," she said, "so rather than coming back here, why don't I
just deliver them to your home? Would that be okay?"

"You'll do that?" I replied. She assured me it would be

her pleasure.

It was 4:00 PM later that day and we were packing when I heard her car drive up. I met Mona at the door. "I'm confident these will fit perfectly." She handed me my new pants on hangers. "But just in case, why don't you try them on. The tailor is available until 9:00 PM."

I hurried back to the bedroom and slid in and out of both pairs and then returned to the front and gave Mona the thumbs-up. She nodded. I shook her hand and expressed my gratitude—she didn't have to do all this, I explained, but I was so grateful she did. I walked her down the drive and she explained that this was her way of doing business. "Todd," she said, "I hope you buy from me for the rest of your life. And Sheryl too. That's very important to me."

I held the driver side open and thanked her again, assuring her we'd ask for her every time. She waved as she backed out of the driveway and I noticed a few other items hanging in plastic in her back seat—more deliveries no doubt. I waved back as she pulled onto our street. As she drove away I caught a glimpse of her personalized license plate. Aptly, it read "SERVE."

LESSON SUMMARY

Good customer service is merely the ante for staying in the game. You must do something more, something that exceeds expectations to continually win the pot. Mona did what she was asked by finding the right pants for me and having them quickly hemmed. What she didn't have to do was bring the pants to our home—on a Sunday, no less. But in the grand scheme, it's a small price she paid to secure our business and the business of our friends for good. Think: How can you or your business go overboard for your customers? Your answer is your best bet for loyal, lucrative sales.

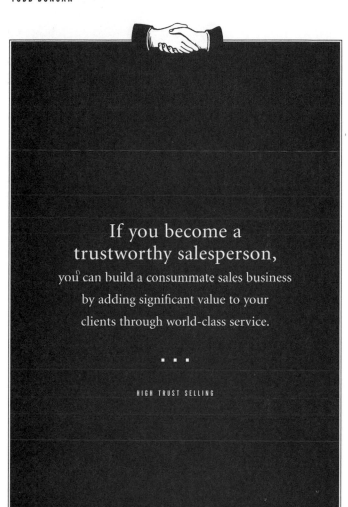

If you become a
trustworthy salesperson,
you can build a consummate sales business
by adding significant value to your
clients through world-class service.

• • •

HIGH TRUST SELLING

Long-term sales success happens
when *high trust* exists—

when you are a trustworthy salesperson

running a trustworthy sales business,

and when it's clear to your clients that you are

a person of integrity who will not only do what

you say but who also has the means to deliver.

■ ■ ■

HIGH TRUST SELLING

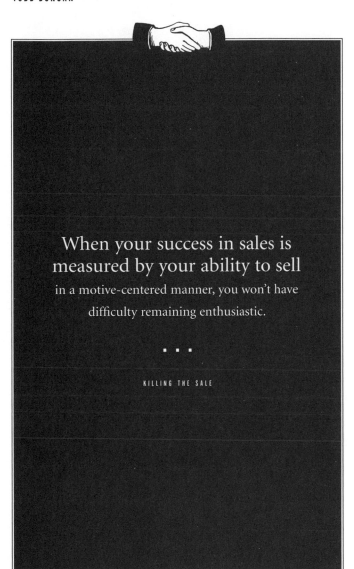

When your success in sales is
measured by your ability to sell
in a motive-centered manner, you won't have
difficulty remaining enthusiastic.

. . .

KILLING THE SALE

GOOD BUSINESS
IS GOOD CONVERSATION

...

Hutchinson, Minnesota, is just south of the middle of the state, about an hour's drive west of the Twin Cities overlooking the Crow River Valley. In summer, folks come from surrounding areas to celebrate the Polka Festival and the Grand Day Parade at the McLeod County Fair. Three lakes sparkle minutes from downtown where fishermen and brave swimmers pass their time and there is green space in abundance for those who enjoy an afternoon nap. Hutchinson is a lovely place to miss the sounds of the big cities but it's an unlikely place for an ambitious mortgage professional to settle down. Ian did anyway.

There are only 13,451 residents in Hutchinson and less than 5,700 homes with an approximate median price of

$115,000. The city limits encompass only 7.4 square miles of space. None of this kept Ian from setting his sights high. Really high. His goal was to gross $35 million in loans that year.

He sat down with a coach and was told it would be impossible without a brilliant strategy. Hutchinson was not the kind of place you could rely on walk-ins or eye-catching billboards. And you could not do all the work yourself. You needed a team to expand your productivity and a network of locals to spread the good word.

Ian got right to work with a two-part plan. He began talking regularly with current customers to make sure he was meeting their needs and then he formed partnerships with influential townsfolk.

You might guess what happened. People started talking and Ian began delivering. Word travels fast in a small town because good business is good conversation. By the end of the year Ian had far surpassed his goal. When the final tally came in, he'd closed over $66 million in loans, nearly double his initial target.

This was two years ago and his business wasn't done climbing.

Ian remains a topic of conversation today and his team averages about $100 million in loans each year. But he quickly explains that numbers no longer matter. Now his goal is simple: to meet the needs of his friends. That's what customers become when you do good business in a small town.

LESSON SUMMARY

Crunch all the numbers you like, small odds of success don't matter when you have a foolproof strategy. Ian knew how word travels in a small town and he came up with a business plan that leveraged its pace. Word-of-mouth marketing is, and probably will remain, the best way to grow a business. The key is giving people a reason to talk without telling them what to say. Do this and it won't matter if the odds aren't in your favor; eventually, everybody acts on what they hear if they hear it enough.

Unwavering sales success
is maintained by consistency.

Consistent actions on your part lead
to consistent expectations on the customer's
part…which lead to consistent reactions
from the customer…which lead to consistent
results in the sales transaction.

■ ■ ■

KILLING THE SALE

How you work where you are
matters more than where
you work.

. .

How you sell what you have
matters more than what
you have to sell.

. .

How you make your calls
matters more than how many
calls you make.

How many hours you produce
matters more than how many
hours you work.

. .

Getting loyal business
matters more than how much
business you get.

. .

Having clients with high trust
matters more than how
many clients you have.

. . .

HIGH TRUST SELLING

SETTING YOUR
OWN STANDARDS

■ ■ ■

During the mid-1950s, Armour and Company was touting Dial as the nation's leading antibacterial bar soap. Their slogan, "Aren't you glad you use Dial? Don't you wish everybody did?" was pasted everywhere—on billboards and buildings, in major newspapers and popular magazines. To compete, in 1958 Proctor & Gamble released its own antibacterial bar called Zest and with it the promise: "For the first time in your life, feel really clean."

When Gary took a job selling P & G soap to hospitals during the height of competition, he knew he was inheriting a good reputation and one of the finest products on the market. But he wasn't confident Zest was the best available.

At the time, the average stay in a hospital was over a week. Gary knew that a priority for hospitals was a soap that could eliminate the spread of bacteria in the most efficient manner. Both Armour and P & G insisted their soap was king but Gary took neither at their word. Instead he set out to do some research of his own.

He drove from Des Moines to Omaha to pay a visit to a leading bacteriologist there. He had only one question: Which soap kills bacteria the best? The doctor had run the tests and he had the answer. With thanks Gary took his answer back home.

For the next fifteen years, Gary enjoyed a successful career selling soap for Proctor & Gamble and each time he met with a hospital executive his pitch was the same. "I spoke with a bacteriologist in Omaha and he assured me that Dial takes two to three days to kill bacteria but Zest kills bacteria immediately."

LESSON SUMMARY

Know your product. Gary could've leaned on the reputation of P&G to sell his wares but he insisted on something stronger. By verifying the singular effectiveness of Zest he not only determined how to set his product apart from the competition, he offered hard evidence that he could be trusted. A salesperson willing to do his own research—and accept the conclusions with integrity—is a salesperson who has his customers' interests in mind.

Become a buyer in your own market. To remain ahead of your competition, you must understand what it's like to be a consumer of your product. You can't truly empathize with your buyers until you are one—otherwise your empathy is really just sympathy.

. . .

KILLING THE SALE

If your goal is to build high trust, a giant step is taken when the features of your product or services are tied to a prospect's intrinsic needs and values.

. . .

HIGH TRUST SELLING

A NEW OUTLOOK

· · ·

Hospitals can open your eyes. Tom found this out when eighty-hour weeks took their toll.

He was a successful salesman and long hours were his leg up. His reward was becoming one of the top salespeople in his industry but it had a high price tag. In 1992, he ended up in the ICU of a local hospital with a brain aneurysm that would need emergency surgery.

While awaiting the operation, Tom battled his compulsion. He picked up his cell and dialed a client's number. He wouldn't lose business because of this. Then a nurse walked by and caught him with the phone to his ear. Incredulous, she approached the bed. His condition was serious, she scolded, and it was critical that he rest. *Critical*. She insisted he stop working or she'd take his phone away.

Tom set his phone on a table and watched the nurse step into the hallway. He then picked it back up. Before he dialed, he paused. He looked around. He saw a hospital bed and a cotton gown. What was he thinking? The nurse was right. This wasn't a laughing matter. What would his family do if he didn't make it? His wife and their two babies—they needed him around.

These thoughts continued as they wheeled him down the white hall. They were still on his mind as the anesthesiologist hovered above him and a warm sensation poured through his body.

When he came to, he was in the ICU again and his head was bandaged and work seemed very different. Once his recovery was complete, Tom hired two assistants and began cutting his hours in half. It made him nervous but he stuck with it. After an initial dip in productivity, business picked back up until it was eventually outpacing its pre-op tempo. Today, Tom's business brings in three times more than before his surgery, proving that more work doesn't always mean more sales.

LESSON SUMMARY

It took a stern nurse and a cold gurney to set Tom straight, but he learned that success is achieved by maintaining priorities, not working harder. By delegating many of his daily tasks to a team of capable people, he freed up his time to solely invest in what he knew best—his customers. This alone brought on satisfaction two-fold: business boomed and he had the time to enjoy its success.

The following are the ten best
investments you can make to reap a more
secure and successful sales business,
as well as a more abundant life.

1. Invest in your relationships with those you love.

2. Invest in a long-term personal-development program.

3. Invest in a sales coach.

4. Invest in a competent right-hand assistant.

5. Invest in your personal image.

6. Invest in a personal financial plan.

7. Invest time in an exercise program.

8. Invest in a client-retention program.

9. Invest in a library.

10. Invest in technology.

▪ ▪ ▪

HIGH TRUST SELLING

CASHING IN ON COMPETITION

• • •

Rivalry happened naturally for Kevin, Ed, and Don—they are friends who sell loans for the same mortgage company. But it wasn't until they changed the face of competition that their careers took off.

At the close of 1995, each had achieved notable levels of success. Kevin closed 102 loans, Don closed 132, and Ed closed 119—all above average for industry standards but all short of personal expectations. Then Ed had an idea. Instead of worrying about end-of-the-year bragging rights, why wouldn't the three help each other take their businesses to the next level? Forget the annual competition for a moment. Didn't they all want to grow their business? Wasn't that the most important thing? This then was how they could do it. They were, after all, friends before they were coworkers.

They put their heads together and came up with a system by which each held the other accountable for setting and meeting weekly sales goals. They granted each other permission to ask for updates and they carved out time for sharing strategic advice. The system became part of their weekly routine and before long they had reason to celebrate.

In 2001, just six years after initiating the strategy, the trio accounted for 65 percent of their company's profit. In that year alone, Kevin closed 283 loans, Don closed 362, and Ed closed 394, thus proving the maxim that *three* heads are better than one.

LESSON SUMMARY

Competition can provide positive pressure but accountability is more effective. When you want to increase your productivity, tell someone you know about it. Give them permission to ask for updates and offer candid advice whenever they see fit. This is especially effective if your accountability comes from the inside. Whenever possible, set up mutual accountability with a colleague whereby each holds the other to meeting his or her goals.

Accountability produces the leverage necessary to follow through with your aspirations.

The right kind of leverage is much more than motivation or hope; it is the essential link between what you desire and what you do, between your dreams and your destiny.

The people with whom you share your aspirations must be the dream stokers in your life; they must be dream makers; they must be people who have hearts for seeing you succeed and hands for helping you do so.

■ ■ ■

HIGH TRUST SELLING

Cease to sell alone by reaching
out to others who will help you succeed
on a level far greater than you can by yourself.
Become more vulnerable in accountability
relationships so that you can be more
valuable in client relationships.
Multiply your partners so that you can
multiply your propensity for success.

■ ■ ■

HIGH TRUST SELLING

SPOILING
THE STATUS QUO

• • •

Sheryl and I were shopping for a Toyota Sequoia and we opted for a dealership close to home. We'd taken one step from our car when we were spotted. From his strategic perch the sales-hawk swooped down on us like we were field mice. "Can I help you with anything?" he squawked. I tried giving him the brush-off but he wouldn't budge. He shadowed us and persisted. Peck, peck, peck. I finally gave in and told him what we were looking for. "We don't have any," he replied. Awkward silence. "Well…are there any in service that we can take a look at?" Again his answer was curt. "We're not allowed to do that." Then, as if he'd done something to earn it, he asked, "If I could locate one for you at another dealership would you buy it now?" Was he kidding? We wiggled free from his talons and jumped in our car.

About an hour away was another dealership and I was nervous the drive wasn't worth it. We were shocked when after several minutes of surveying the lot, no one had approached us. We didn't spot any Sequoias so we headed to the showroom where Bill smiled and shook our hands. He admitted they too were out of Sequoias and asked if we'd be interested in learning a little more about them before we continued our search. It was a good idea and nice of him to offer.

For the next thirty minutes Bill answered our questions unassumingly, helping us customize a car to our needs. When we finished he asked if we'd like him to check their inventory to determine when one might be in. Sure, we said. He returned shortly. "The soonest we can have your car here is three weeks. If you'd like, I can reserve it for you with no obligation to purchase it." Waiting three weeks wasn't ideal but Bill had helped us. We told him it sounded good and he secured the order.

Over the next three weeks, we kept looking and found a dealership a little closer to home with a suitable Sequoia on the lot. We even test drove it but when it came time to close the deal we declined. We wanted to give our business to Bill. He'd earned our trust and we knew he wouldn't let us down.

Three weeks later we used two train tickets he'd purchased for us and made our way to meet him. Bill picked us up at the station and drove us to the lot where our car was waiting. It was just as we wanted it and we were glad for Bill's sake that we had waited. He rewrote the selling script and deserved our business. Now we'll never buy a Toyota from anyone else.

LESSON SUMMARY

Sometimes all that's required is spoiling the status quo. The sales profession has the reputation for being slimy and seedy. Often, being yourself and acting out the golden rule is the simplest form of salesmanship. Coincidentally, it's also the most lucrative.

Prospects don't respond
well to people who sound as
if they're selling something.

They respond to people who are courteous and

genuine—people who are just regular people—

people they could see themselves befriending.

■ ■ ■

KILLING THE SALE

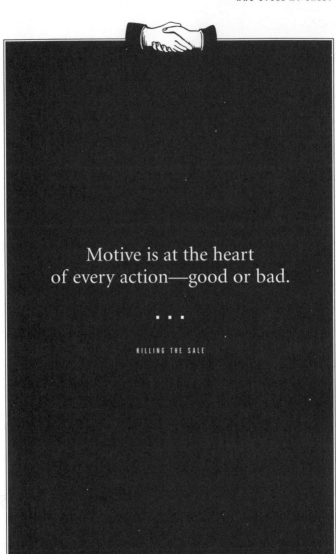

Motive is at the heart
of every action—good or bad.

■ ■ ■

KILLING THE SALE

The right questions—
and an actively listening ear—will help you
understand prospects' core values and real needs,
ideally putting you in a position to
add value with your product where value
is both wanted and needed most.

. . .

KILLING THE SALE

THE VALUE
OF FOCUSED TIME

■ ■ ■

Linda calls it "the best business decision" she's ever made. Work had become a burden. She was spending most of her time filing paperwork, filling out forms, crunching numbers, and fidgeting with broken technology. When she tallied the time she'd been spending on nonselling tasks, the numbers were staggering. Five hours a week at the photocopier. Four hours a week at the fax machine. Five hours a week reading and sending emails. Twenty hours a week on unnecessary phone calls.

All totaled, she was spending about thirty-four hours a week doing nothing but administrative tasks. In her efforts to become a successful saleswoman she'd become an administrative assistant. That wasn't the plan.

The worst part was that she was not the only one suffering. Her clients were not receiving her full attention and she didn't want to think about what that meant.

This was when her superwoman mentality seemed foolish. She decided to put a stop to what she called her "ego thing" and begin relying on her team. They stood willing to help all along and when given the opportunity they turned out to be far more capable than she realized.

The following year, having delegated all tasks but building relationships with customers, Linda's business grew by 183 percent. It's astounding what can happen when a salesperson stays focused on relationships, and trusts others to carry the bulk of the load.

LESSON SUMMARY

If you're a salesperson, focus your efforts on selling, not on paperwork or administration. Focus your talents on that which you do best and let others take care of the rest.

Slowing down, making observations, and if necessary, charting a more profitable course of action is a hallmark trait of all top-producing, trustworthy salespeople.

■ ■ ■

HIGH TRUST SELLING

Delegation to the
right people makes everything easier,
not only on the job but also in your life.

. . .

KILLING THE SALE

TAKING RESPONSIBILITY

. . .

A few years ago I ordered twelve Mylar balloons—my wife's favorite—along with a single rose to be delivered the morning of her birthday. I wanted to begin her day with a bang. Imagine my surprise when I returned from the office the day before and my wife thanked me for her balloons. I hugged her and told her she was welcome and then went on with our evening never acknowledging the surprise was premature.

As we climbed into bed that night I glanced at the balloons and the bunch looked a little thin. I counted with my eyes and there were only six. I was letting the day-early delivery slide—but getting half of what I paid for? Now that was a problem.

I called the flower company from work the following

morning and explained the mistake. Connor immediately took the blame. "Mr. Duncan," she said, "that is completely unacceptable and not the way we do business. I take full responsibility. Tell me what needs to happen so you will feel good about your choice to use our services."

"Well," I replied, "I really don't want to pay for something I didn't get. And if I'm being honest, I'm a little annoyed the delivery was a day early."

"You're right," Connor replied. "You shouldn't have to pay for something you didn't get so I am refunding your card right now for the six missing balloons. And because we delivered them a day early, we'd like to pay for your next delivery if you'll let us. Is there another special occasion coming up?"

Valentine's Day, I told her, and then she set up my order free of charge. She then asked for my permission to arrange two more deliveries at no obligation to me. "We will email you an automatic reminder when the day is approaching," she explained, "and then you can decide if you want to follow through with the delivery." Wise move.

Since that day, I have used Connor's services more than a dozen times. It's refreshing to come across a salesperson who takes responsibility for her company's reputation.

LESSON SUMMARY

Reputation is more than a consistent smile and handshake. Reputation precedes us into every sales encounter. It often predetermines a customer's attitude and is a main factor that makes or breaks the deal. Take your reputation seriously; it's not something that's easily altered.

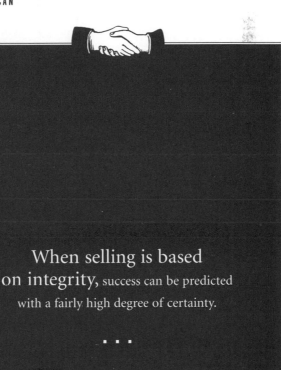

When selling is based
on integrity, success can be predicted
with a fairly high degree of certainty.

■ ■ ■

KILLING THE SALE

Salespeople who focus
only on customer *acquisition*
don't remain on top for long.
It's those with high customer *retention*
who rule the roost.

■ ■ ■

KILLING THE SALE

Trust must be at the core of
any and every client relationship
in order for you to realize full lifetime
value of every client.

. . .

KILLING THE SALE

COURTESY CLOSED THE DEAL

. . .

It was the kind of place where salespeople took turns approaching walk-ins. A customer would push through the glass doors innocently, wanting nothing more than a look inside, and within thirty seconds someone was on him asking tired questions.

They'd visited the place before—this young couple in the market for a new sofa—and an unrelenting salesman shadowed them from a distance of fifty feet. He thought they wouldn't notice—thought they would think he was checking price tags or something—but they noticed and now they were defensive.

They wore game faces as they pushed through the glass doors this time. Then the couple noticed Marsha near the front of the store. "Don't make eye contact," the wife whispered out of the side of her mouth. Marsha only said hello and gave a considerate nod.

The couple continued their search without distraction and when they discovered the perfect sofa they sought out Marsha to ask her opinion. "What is your home like?" she asked. They explained and she made a suggestion. "What I would do is jot down the measurements of the sofa and then when you get home, fold a sheet to the same size and lay it in the space you intend to put the sofa. Walk around it a few days and see how it feels.

"I wouldn't take anything home today if I were you," she continued. "I'd give the sheet-thing a try and if it works, come back on a Saturday when the reduced warehouse is stocked. There are great deals all the time."

The couple asked Marsha if she worked on Saturdays and she said only once a month. They then took her advice with thanks and went home with only a piece of paper and some scribbled measurements.

Two Saturday's later Marsha was on the schedule and the couple returned and bought three items instead of one, demonstrating that courtesy often fosters the greatest return.

LESSON SUMMARY

Always be courteous. You never know when it will be the little thing that makes a big difference. The couple shopping for a sofa expected discourtesy and pushiness and when their expectations didn't match with the reality Marsha created, they were immediately drawn to her. Courtesy will close many deals if you will just be patient.

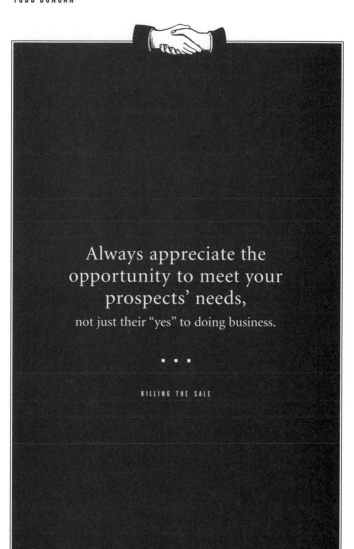

Always appreciate the
opportunity to meet your
prospects' needs,

not just their "yes" to doing business.

. . .

KILLING THE SALE

A vital part of selling
is asking the right questions
so that what you sell and what a client
wants match up. In other words, the key
to selling is not selling, it is providing.
And the key to providing is
knowing in advance what to provide.

■ ■ ■

HIGH TRUST SELLING

When your authentic actions
create an environment that breeds
buy-in with your prospects,
closing sales tends to become an afterthought.
It will be the natural conclusion to your
prospect interactions and the natural beginning
to your client relationships.

■ ■ ■

HIGH TRUST SELLING

THE
SOUTHERN WAY

...

A couple wanted to stretch their dollars, but southern California was not the place to do it. They spent hours looking at homes online in three other states and came across a beautiful place in Georgia. Business would take them to the area the following month so they arranged with the realtor to tour the home then.

Three weeks later, they met her in a parking lot and hopped into her car. Nancy showed them the house and then eleven others. She wanted to give them a true feel for what their dollars could buy in her town and she sensed they could do even better than the house they had originally come to see.

After the first day the couple was in love with a restored nineteenth century farmhouse on two-and-a-half acres. It was the most expensive of the twelve homes they toured and also the smallest. This didn't sit right with Nancy. She asked them to consider looking at a few more homes before making a final decision. She had a feeling about one home they had not yet seen. The couple agreed.

The following morning on the way to the first home, Nancy handed them each a color flyer. "Here's where we're headed." The picture was of a large Cape Cod in a wooded neighborhood. The lot was beautifully landscaped and bordered by a 500-acre nature preserve. At the bottom of the flyer was the asking price: $70,000 less than the farmhouse. When the three walked through the front door they sighed in unison. It was the one. Their offer was accepted that afternoon.

As an early celebration, Nancy treated the couple to dinner at her favorite restaurant where the owner and the cook knew her by name. The couple received warm welcomes and complimentary sweet tea. It was the perfect ending to an exciting day.

To show their gratitude the couple made plans to buy Nancy dinner once they returned to sign the final paperwork. She graciously accepted and then outdid them like they do in the South. She had an eight-acre farm, she explained, and a finished barn where they would stay when they arrived back in town. She insisted and so began a dear friendship.

Not long after they moved, the couple referred some friends to Nancy and she worked her magic again. Now the five of them share dinner once a month at Nancy's farm, proving there's something endearing and enduring about doing business the Southern way.

LESSON SUMMARY

The Southern way is simple: treat customers like friends and their friends will become your customers. The story doesn't end there. Since their regular dinners, the two couples each referred Nancy two more couples. This means her considerate ways earned her a five-fold increase in business from one customer. That's about the way it works when you do business the Southern way.

To be a successful sales professional,
you must *establish* trust with your
prospects so that they become clients.
You must also *foster* their trust so that
they *remain* clients.

■ ■ ■

KILLING THE SALE

To be a top-notch salesperson,
you need to be selling solutions to
your prospects' deepest needs.
You need to be selling the fulfillment
of your prospects' deepest desires.

■ ■ ■

HIGH TRUST SELLING

The salesperson who
adds value after the sale
clearly demonstrates that the relationship
is more important than revenue,
and the person is more important than profits.

■ ■ ■

HIGH TRUST SELLING

SUCCESS IS
YOUR BUSINESS

• • •

Jean began her second stint as a sales professional in 1992, at the age of fifty-four. She had some success her first go-around but it had been eleven years since she'd called on a client and even longer since she'd built a sales business from scratch.

Initially, she went about things the way most ambitious salespeople do—she put in a lot of hard hours to maximize the few resources her employer offered. Fifty and sixty hour weeks were common. She was met with some success but not enough. Something else was required.

Late in that first year, she spent her own money to attend a seminar that she hoped would show her what more was needed. There she learned about something I call "The Law of the Shareholder." Like any start-up, her business would grow when she invested in it.

She had taken one step in the right direction by attending the seminar. Now, her next investment was to hire a coach—this too with her own money. It was a risk but one she was willing to take. It turned out to be a wise move.

Her coach helped her see that she was still looking at herself as an employee rather than the owner of a business. If her second career was to succeed she needed to begin acting like its CEO. The advice clicked.

The two then put together a business plan that determined what investments were necessary, initially and continually, for her second career to flourish. She took ownership and began to put these investments of time and money to practice: they included professional marketing, ongoing coaching, professional growth materials, and affiliate partnerships. Within a year both business and life began to change.

Today, a decade later, Jean is not only the owner of the company in principle, it says so on her business card. This allows her the freedom to spend only thirty hours a week in the office, and leaves her plenty of time for her growing family. In fact, her business is also a family affair. Her son is now the executive vice president and her daughter a top salesperson. So much for the adage that you can't mix business and pleasure.

LESSON SUMMARY

You are the owner of your business whether or not your card says so. You are responsible for your success. You must make the ongoing decisions necessary to launch and continually grow your business or no one will. See yourself as the CEO of "You, Inc." and you will begin to see success in the proper light.

The greatest salespeople see the
summit of success as a product
of continually improving,
continually honing the tools of their trade,
continually raising the bar in their chosen field.

■ ■ ■

HIGH TRUST SELLING

The most successful sales
people by stock in themselves.
That begins when you stop thinking of
yourself as an employee with a job and start
thinking of yourself as an owner of a business
with a compelling vision to help people.

■ ■ ■

HIGH TRUST SELLING

Take initiative to invest
(your own money if you have to)
in a professional coach or mentor whose
goal is to help you bridge the gap between
your dreams and destiny.

■ ■ ■

HIGH TRUST SELLING

CLEANING UP YOUR TIME

. . .

When Tim began tallying the amount of time he spent on various tasks at work, he figured it would help him recapture thirty-or-so minutes a day. He would stop piddling so much and head home a little earlier and this was a small victory. He had no idea what he was talking about.

When Tim tallied the amount of time he stood at the fax machine over the course of three weeks and then multiplied that number over the course of a year, the figure he came up with was staggering and had to be wrong. He rechecked his log and punched in the numbers again. Same result. Unbelievable.

At his current pace, Tim found out he was spending approximately 336 hours at the fax machine every year. In eight-hour increments, this came to forty-two work days.

The fax machine wasn't that important.

He had intended this little exercise to be an encouragement but it had blown up in his face. Now he had to deal with the knowledge that he spent about one-fifth of his work time sending faxes, watching faxes be sent, waiting for confirmations, and refaxing misfaxes. He had to face up the fact that he was a major time waster. This wasn't part of his plan—but now he had to do something about it.

Tim thought for a few days and then went to his boss and proposed a deal. He would hire an assistant with his own money in order to free up his time to invest in customer relations. If this move proved to increase his revenue enough to cover the assistant's salary by the end of six months, the company would take over her salary and he would reap the additional profits. His boss agreed.

Two months into the deal, Tim's refocused time was already generating enough additional revenue to cover his assistant's salary. Four months later, his company took over the expense.

It had worked so well for Tim that he hired a second assistant, then a third. Today, Tim has a dozen assistants that run the business for him. He works eighty days a year and his business annually takes in between eighty to one hundred million dollars in revenue. Cleaning up your time can reap major rewards.

LESSON SUMMARY

We all waste time at work—it's just a matter of how much. Chances are good that if you're in sales, you're wasting about three-fourths of your working hours. Tally your time on daily tasks for a week to know for sure. If, like Tim, you find you are faxing your career away, delegate your tasks to an assistant; and if your company will not provide one, share an assistant with a co-worker until your increase in revenue pays for you to have your own. This will only be the beginning of freeing up your time.

You could spend more time
doing the things that advance
your career if you could get rid of the
things that are holding you back.

■ ■ ■

HIGH TRUST SELLING

When you know the value
of an hour of your time,
your job is then to never spend time
on a task that produces less than you're worth,
now or in the future.

■ ■ ■

HIGH TRUST SELLING

Consider how things would be
different if you were actually able
to spend all of your time doing the few things
that you enjoy most that produce the greatest
impact on your business.

■ ■ ■

HIGH TRUST SELLING

UNFLEXING YOUR MUSCLES

● ● ●

I suppose it was my dad who first introduced me to the concept of muscling when I was still young. He understood how to avoid it. I, on the other hand, was a boy, and I didn't understand things as he did. Like many salespeople, I had to learn things the hard way.

I must have been about ten years old when I spent some time at work with my dad one afternoon, observing his responsibilities as a doctor. I remember being fascinated by the idea of a giant camera taking X-ray pictures of people's insides.

X-ray vision was, of course, a necessary skill for every superhero if he was good for anything. And the thought that my father had access to such a skill was thrilling. There was a problem however and it was that he was a radiologist.

He only read the X-rays; he didn't take them.

"Dad," I asked with an incredulous look, "why don't *you* take the pictures?" Surely, he would want to take advantage of such an extraordinary skill.

"Son," he replied, "I get paid to read the X-rays."

It was a significant point to consider. It's too bad his wisdom didn't readily sink in back then. If I'd been a little wiser I might have saved myself a lot of frustration and failure in my selling career.

Whether or not he knew it, my dad's response that day indicated that he was very clear about his responsibilities. As a radiologist my father knew that certain tasks were productive, and others were not—even if they could be viewed as part of the radiology process. In short, he understood his job description. Something many salespeople don't seem to readily comprehend until it's too late. Until they are a salesperson, secretary, courier, copier, filer, faxer, computer-repair technician, and social-activities director in one. Until their sales job is no longer a job for one; it's a job for ten—still being carried out by one very weary person. Have you ever felt overwhelmed with your "responsibilities?" Maybe it's time to unflex your muscles and use them for what matters most.

LESSON SUMMARY

You are a salesperson, which is to say you are paid to make sales. There are two tasks that fall into this category: 1) building trust with new prospects, and 2) fostering trust with existing customers. The more time you spend on these two tasks, the more successful you will be.

Muscling is overestimating the value of doing

and underestimating the value of delegation.
It's doing everything in the
selling process yourself—
whether it is necessary that you do it—
and delegating nothing.

■ ■ ■

HIGH TRUST SELLING

KNOW YOUR PRODUCT WELL; KNOW YOUR CUSTOMERS BETTER

. . .

When I spoke with my friend Mike a few years ago, I was logging thousands of air miles a year. I was looking for one company to handle all of my ongoing travel needs and he knew the owner of a successful travel agency. Following our conversation, Mike arranged a meeting between the owner and me.

As a consumer, I am always open to exploring new ways to maximize the value of money that I exchange for goods and services. In this particular case, I was not only looking for new ways to stretch my traveling dollars; I was looking for innovative ways to shrink my traveling time. When the owner and I sat down, I was eager to share my most important value and needs. I wanted him to know that being home was more important than being on the road; I would spend more money on a direct flight if it got me home sooner. I was anxious to have a personalized agency that understood me.

Unfortunately, ninety seconds into our meeting, he had already lost my business.

He began with these words: "Todd, I'd like to tell you a little about our company." And away he went. For nearly twenty minutes he told me how the agency began, how much business it was doing, and why he felt I should use the agency. He then launched in to a showering of features and benefits like the CD-ROM that I would receive every quarter with listings of hotels and restaurants. He told me about the toll-free line should any needs arise, and the emergency hotline, should I ever get stuck. He explained the quarterly reports to help me manage my travel expenses. On and on he went, pontificating about the things he thought I wanted. Finally, he said, they would make me an unlimited supply of luggage tags.

Then came the classic line: "Todd, we'd like to ask you for your business."

Isn't that what we have been taught to do? Ask for business?

With my arms crossed, I replied, "I'm not very motivated to give it to you."

"I could tell," he replied.

"For how long could you tell?"

"About five minutes into our dialogue."

"That's the problem," I explained. "We haven't had a dialogue."

He looked at me confused.

I then asked him a series of questions to demonstrate what I meant: "What's my favorite airline? What's my favorite hotel? What kind of bed do I prefer? Do I like top floors or bottom floors? Near the elevator or in a corner? Smoking or non-smoking? Who pays for my travel—me or my clients? What times of day do I prefer to travel? And how many luggage tags do I already own?"

I admit, I was overdoing it but he got the point. He knew nothing about my personal values, my travel needs, or what was important to me about a relationship with a travel agency. After nearly half an hour of stating his case, he knew nothing that he needed to know in order to close the deal. I didn't need the financial reports or the list of hotels and restaurants. I wouldn't use the hotline. And as a frequent flyer on several airlines, I already owned plenty of luggage tags.

He started the meeting talking when he should have been ready to listen. It is often the main difference between shooting in the dark and confidently closing the deal.

LESSON SUMMARY

In basic terms, the mistake is something I call arguing. It's talking too much and listening too little, if at all. It's staking your sales success on your ability to state your case in convincing fashion. It's mastering a monologue and then expecting the jury of your prospects to take your side. But arguing only makes certain your sales get a death sentence. The reason is simple: You can't build trust with a prospect if you're the only one talking. Establishing an initial level of trust takes more than flowery monologue. It takes dialogue. It takes actual conversation. There is no other way for you to know that your product or service will meet a prospect's needs.

You can't build trust
with a prospect if you're the only one talking.

■ ■ ■

KILLING THE SALE

By taking the time to listen
(and showing prospects that is your intention),
you avoid monopolizing the conversation
with empty sales talk.

■ ■ ■

KILLING THE SALE

THE END OF COLD CALLING

. . .

When 9:00 AM rolled around, Brent was raring to go. With his list of banks and managers' names in hand, he pulled out a *Thomas Guide* and mapped the most efficient route to call on as many locations as possible. It was his first day of selling but he was confident his efforts would reap some business.

By ten o'clock, he stepped out of his car and walked to the front doors of a bank that he knew didn't offer loans to individuals with poor credit. As good a place to start as any.

Wearing his best smile, he pushed through the doors and presented himself to the receptionist. She looked at him with a blank stare and said nothing. After ten awkward seconds she gathered herself and asked for Brent to repeat the name of the gentleman. He repeated it and she replied that he wasn't there.

"Can I leave him my card and some information?"

The receptionist fumbled with her words. "Um...how long...have you been working with him?"

"I just left him a voice mail last week and I'm stopping buy to discuss some potential business."

This time she asked Brent to wait at the front while she excused herself. Two minutes later, she returned with one of the prospect's coworkers. The man's face was drawn. He asked again for clarification and Brent repeated his answer.

Subtly, the man lowered his head. "I'm sorry to have to tell you this, but he passed away on Saturday of a heart attack."

LESSON SUMMARY

For Brent, the experience was a harsh and tragic introduction to the world of selling. It's one, however, that he could have avoided. When I began selling, a mentor taught me three lessons about prospecting that I have always tried to model: 1) Never call on prospects who don't know you're calling, 2) Never call on prospects that aren't excited to have you call, and 3) Never leave a prospect without adding more value that you have received.

If you want to convey trust,

don't ever assume prospects have time to talk to
you. Schedule only what you intend to maintain.
Call only when your prospect expects it.

■ ■ ■

KILLING THE SALE

If you don't have an effective,
efficient plan for selling,
any business you get is accidental.

■ ■ ■

HIGH TRUST SELLING

If you've done the preliminary
work of ascertaining your
prospects' values and needs,
and you are confident that your product
or service can fulfill them, your sales
presentation should be like offering
a well-thought-out gift to a friend.

■ ■ ■

HIGH TRUST SELLING

LET DIALOGUE
OPEN DOORS

■ ■ ■

When Dave and I arrived at the prospect's corporate offices, we were escorted into the top-floor conference room. Shortly thereafter, the prospects' representatives filed in stiffly and silently and we felt like two criminals under a single bulb. All eyes focused on us and their smiles were as straight as their suits. Without a word, Dave and I knew our customary prospecting approach had become all the more important. These were straight shooters and we needed to stick to our guns.

Since they saw this as an interview of us, we exchanged a few pleasantries before the head of production said, "So tell us about the Duncan Group."

It was our moment of truth and for some a perfect opportunity to do some professional bragging. Fortunately, we didn't see it this way.

"Thanks for asking," I replied. "The Duncan Group is many things to many companies. Our overarching goal is to help our clients and their employees become more successful through our training partnerships and programs." I then paused. "But we can't even begin to explain how we might do that for you until we learn what's important to you about this training program."

It was the key and for forty-five minutes we then dialogued about their needs and values. At the end of this time, we told them how we thought we could help and they responded that they liked what they heard and would be in touch in two weeks.

On our way out, Dave and I wrote six thank-you cards and dropped them in the mailbox on the first floor and then we waited anxiously for the phone to ring.

Like clockwork, a spokesperson for the prospect called exactly two weeks from our meeting date to tell us that our company had been awarded the six-figure contract. Since we always ask clients why they choose us, Dave posed the same question to this client.

"You seemed to be the only company that knew what we were looking for," the rep explained. "The others told us what they *thought* they could do for us, but none of it really seemed to fit. You understood where we are coming from."

Never make assumptions. No matter how well you've prequalified your prospect, selling situations are not the place for monologues. Ask questions; ascertain *their* answers. Let dialogue open doors for you.

To communicate trust to
your prospects,
don't ever go into a selling situation
assuming you know what they need.
Let them tell you what is relevant.
Make listening your first priority when you
deal with prospects.

■ ■ ■

KILLING THE SALE

To truly enter into a dialogue
in which you begin to relate to your prospects
on a level that will build trust
(and subsequently close sales), you have to be
willing to put your agenda aside.

■ ■ ■

KILLING THE SALE

When you enter into a selling dialogue, do so with a disciplined set of questions that you've planned ahead of time. Ask questions that will help you determine whether your product or service is the right fit. Determine what your prospects are looking for, why they're looking for it, how they expect it to benefit their lives and their businesses, and when they expect to have it.

. . .

KILLING THE SALE

LESS RESPONSIBILITY MEANS MORE PRODUCTIVITY

. . .

Before cell phones were commonplace, Harry attended one of our events and strategically claimed a seat near the back doors of the conference hall to ensure he was the first person to the pay phone during the breaks. His strategy worked and he spent most if not all of the down time between sessions on the phone with prospects and customers. He couldn't spare a moment. Time was money.

Then, according to Harry, it was in a "blinding flash of the obvious" that his liberation came. As the morbid truths of workaholism were being discussed from stage, he realized that his obsessive-compulsive behavior had put him on the fast track to career atrophy. Not only that, he'd been grossly wasting his resources.

When he returned to work, he immediately determined

what he could delegate to the team he already had in place. There were four of them, self-dubbed "Team Gordon," and they quickly jumped in to help.

For a week, Harry asked them to shadow him throughout the day in order to learn the ropes. It wasn't much longer before all four could handle every task that might arise.

Today, Team Gordon essentially runs the ship. They keep Harry apprised of necessary information by way of Monday morning meetings while he focuses on building deeper relationships with their customers. This simple responsibility affords him a relatively stress-free forty-hour-a-week job that grosses about one hundred million dollars a year in sales—a 400 percent increase from his preliberation total. That's what is called maxing your potential without taxing your life.

LESSON SUMMARY

The mistake that Harry was making is a common one: he was convinced he was the best person for every part of his job. Unless your business runs itself, that is almost never the case. In most industries, you have one major responsibility and several minor ones. The problem is that the more responsibilities you have, the less productive you become. The flip side should be your goal. Take on less responsibility and see more productivity.

Selling is what you do
in the process of living.

It's not the other way around.

Life does not happen after work is done.

Living is supposed to be supported

and supplemented by selling.

Therefore, you must adopt your selling

endeavors to your most treasured life.

■ ■ ■

KILLING THE SALE

Delegation to the right people
makes everything easier,
not only on the job but also in your life.

∎ ∎ ∎

KILLING THE SALE

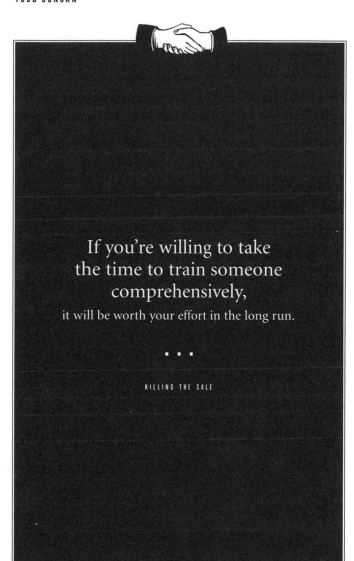

If you're willing to take
the time to train someone
comprehensively,

it will be worth your effort in the long run.

. . .

KILLING THE SALE

SCALING DOWN FOR SUCCESS

. . .

In the popular film, *Jerry Maguire,* Tom Cruise plays a thirty-five-year-old sports agent who can no longer stand himself. With seventy-two athletes in his fold and an average of 264 calls a day, he doesn't have time to listen to his clients. He has become concerned about one thing only: the bottom line. As the movie begins, the narrator (Maguire) explains how he finally reached the breaking point.

He began to notice that "in the quest for the big dollar, a lot of little things were going wrong." His motives gave rise to self-doubt. Was he "just another shark in a suit?"

Then, at a corporate gathering in Miami, he has a breakthrough. He realizes that he hates his place in the world. He'd become the very thing he never set out to be. He was no longer his father's son. In response, and in a moment of hotel room lucidity, he sets out to write a mission statement. He titles it: "The Things We Think and Do Not Say: The Future of Our Business."

In it, Maguire details the basics of his job—the "simple pleasures." He recalls the words of his mentor. Personal relationships are the key to business. He writes and writes until it all comes out. In the end, he comes to a conclusion: Fewer clients. Less money. More attention. He runs to the Copymat in the middle of the night and makes 110 copies for everyone in his office.

If you've seen the film, you know that Maguire is fired shortly after distributing his "mission statement." In an awkward-but-passionate display, he vows to his boss and coworkers that he will succeed despite them.

In one of the final scenes, redemption comes. Maguire, with tears in his eyes, embraces his only client (played by Cuba Gooding, Jr.) who has just played the game of his life. Looking on is his former boss, Bob Sugar, with one of his clients. The client turns to Sugar with an earnest look and asks, "Why don't we have a relationship like that?"

LESSON SUMMARY

It takes time to develop a relationship, but if that's not your goal with every customer then you will always be forced to rely on new business in order to stay afloat. What would you like your workday to look like: spent investing in people you already know or spent trying to earn the trust of people you don't?

It doesn't matter how many prospects you see.

It matters how you see the right prospects. To maximize your prospecting efficiency you must replace the traditional "more is better" quantity concept with a "less is best" quality concept.

■ ■ ■

HIGH TRUST SELLING

Determine which 20 percent
of your clients yield most
of your profits, and spend the majority
of your time building high trust relationships
with them and those they refer to you.

. . .

KILLING THE SALE

Building lifetime
relationships with every client
must be your goal. And the only way to do that is
to communicate trust consistently
to every one of your clients on a regular basis.

■ ■ ■

KILLING THE SALE

ESTABLISHING THE VALUE OF YOUR TIME

• • •

To be a highly successful salesperson, you must envision your goals for the future of your business. One of those goals should have to do with the volume of sales you expect to receive. To set this goal, you must understand the value of your time, one hour at a time.

Professionals from lawyers to mechanics to computer technicians know the value of an hour's worth of work. And so do you if you hire one. Why? Because the value of each service is quantified with an hourly rate.

For example, when you hire a mechanic to install new brakes, you going to pay not only for the parts but also for the number of hours the car must be serviced. And as we all know, the longer the work takes, the more expensive the service becomes. In fact, in many cases the cost for the service is higher than the cost of the parts. That's because a mechanic's time is more valuable than the parts he sells. A mechanic understands that without his time, parts don't have much value to you.

Therein lies the beauty in this exchange (if you're the mechanic, that is). If the mechanic—who let's say is the best in town—wants to charge you one hundred dollars an hour for his time, he can. Without him you just have a bunch of brake parts and a car that won't stop—two things that do you no good if you don't know how to put them together. Of course, it's your prerogative to take your business elsewhere. But if you want first-class work, it's going to cost you one hundred dollars an hour. That's what this mechanic has determined his time is worth. Will he work on your car for less? No, because there are always people with car troubles who will agree to the value he has placed on his time—especially if they've used his services before.

The bottom line is that the one-hundred-dollar-an-hour mechanic doesn't do cheap work because his time is more valuable than that. Furthermore, he doesn't waste his time because it has a real dollar value. We should all heed this bit of blue collar wisdom because the more time is worth, the less we tend to waste.

LESSON SUMMARY

Think of your job. Would your customers say that the time you give them is more valuable than the product you provide? Do you fill your work hours with activities that increase the value of your time? Or does the value of your time diminish the busier you get? Determine the real value of an hour of your time and it will change how you do business and who you do it with.

When you frame your working days with a predetermined hourly rate that complements both your business and life plans, you will begin to maximize the twenty-four hours you've been given each day.

■ ■ ■

HIGH TRUST SELLING

Working toward earning
your hourly rate every day
means analyzing each task that a client
or potential client might require of you
during the course of your day.

■ ■ ■

HIGH TRUST SELLING

When you know the value
of an hour of your time,

your job is then to never spend time

on a task that produces less than you're worth,

now or in the future.

■ ■ ■

HIGH TRUST SELLING

POWER TO PULL
YOU THROUGH

■ ■ ■

The person who interviewed you for your first sales job probably asked you something like, "Why do you want this job?" Think back. What was your response?

You probably didn't say, "I want to get rich and buy lots of expensive things." You were probably more clever than that, whether or not you meant what you said. It's likely you responded with something to the effect of, "I like helping people."

Why do we say that? Is it because we feel we should, or do we know deep down that helping people is the highest calling of the sales professional?

This brings up an important point about staying motivated to sell. I tend to think that the "I like helping people" answer is not a phony one when we initially give it. I also tend to think that it's easy to forget that answer when things are either going very well or very poorly. However, it's one of the few thoughts that should never leave our minds.

When too much time has passed between sales, it's easy to put profits before people. It's easier to put on an act and attempt to convince people of needs they don't have—to offer them Band-Aid solutions rather than real remedies.

On the other hand, when sales are pouring in it's easier to mash the cruise control and let the customer relationships that got you there slide a little. When you have earned a customer's trust, it's easy to take the relationship for granted.

In either scenario, it's equally crucial to remember what motivated you in the first place so that you don't fall into the traps of deception or delusion. I call such motivation "pull power." It is the antithesis of willpower which is self-generated energy that produces short-term accomplishment.

To make use of pull power in your career you must always keep the reason you sell on the forefront of your mind where it can dictate your decisions and actions. In short, you must never forget *why* you are doing what you're doing. Once this thought is firmly established, it becomes a force that pulls you along in good times, average times, and bad times. Pull power becomes you inner accountability of the deeper reason you are selling.

Many sales professionals get ahead of themselves in this regard. They spend the better part of their days answering the "How" questions: "How can I make more sales? How can I make more money? How will I meet my quota?" They're all good questions that have their place but answering them is not where a successful sales career begins. It's not enough to know *how* to be a good salesperson. To become successful for the long term, in high and calm seas, you must also know *why* you sell. And then never forget it.

LESSON SUMMARY

If you're just in sales for the money, the statistics show that you probably won't make it very far. You'll either quit in three years or less or you'll accept a mediocre career in which stress and disappointment are commonplace. Very few in it for only the money have the nerve to push themselves past the tough times. Determine the deepest reason why you enjoy selling and then let that be the force that compels you to succeed. It's often the only force strong enough to weather the rough seas that will come.

Selling success begins
by determining your higher
purpose in the sales profession.
Your foundational purpose is
your core motivation for thought and action
in every area of your job
your deepest inspiration for getting things done
your critical filter for decision making
your built-in accountability

■ ■ ■

HIGH TRUST SELLING

Once you identify your
purpose with regard to success
and your sales career and begin to align that
purpose with your activities and goals,
you create what's called pull power,
which is the greatest motivating force
for the work you perform. Pull power is
your inner accountability, your constant
reminder, from the heart,
of the deeper reason you are selling.

■ ■ ■

HIGH TRUST SELLING

PROFITABLE RELATIONSHIPS MATURE OVER TIME

• • •

Consider a dating analogy. How many stories have you heard of men who invested a lot of creativity and energy into captivating a beautiful woman in order to win one date with her? Those stories are fairly common, aren't they? And so are sales appointments. But if you asked the guy pursuing the woman if he thought he'd reached his goal by landing one date with her, he'd probably be quick to correct you. Getting her to say yes to a date is just the first step—albeit an important one—if the goal is long-term relationship.

Beyond that first date, additional steps must be taken to grow the relationship, steps that will ultimately determine whether the two will get married one day. Furthermore, once the two are married, that's only the beginning. Beyond marriage vows the couple must decide what is necessary to ensure the continued success of the marriage. And in the end, the man who wins the woman's heart for good—and vice versa—is the one whose actions have consistently fostered the trust that was established on those first few dates.

Relationships that are fruitful and enduring are not comprised of parties committed to only perseverance. If that were true the national divorce rate wouldn't be nearly 60 percent. The most productive relationships are comprised of parties committed to consistently adding value where value is most needed. Think of it this way: a girl doesn't stay with a guy because she's overwhelmed by his persistence; she ultimately stays with him because of the value he adds to her life, and the value she adds to his. This same dynamic is no less apparent in business relationships.

The process of dating, marrying and remaining married is the process of mutually adding value to each other for the long haul. If you remember this in your business relationships, you will become more patient in reaping the benefits from a customer and much less likely to accept anyone into your fold of clientele.

LESSON SUMMARY

There are several creative tricks to getting a sales relationship started—many of which are borderline deceptive—but when it comes to keeping a sales relationship going strong, there are no substitutions for a consistent, value-adding strategy whereby the customer comes to know that she is more important to you that her money. This kind of customer will be glad to remain by your side.

Incubation is the process
by which you consistently add value
to a client for as long as you do
business together, knowing that over time
this will ensure the relationship
matures to fruition.

■ ■ ■

HIGH TRUST SELLING

High trust sales professionals have a different strategy than their counterparts.

A salesperson who focuses on increasing
client share strives to tap the full value of
every client he or she obtains.
He is less concerned about increasing his client
database because he understands that once
he has earned trust with a client,
seeking repeat and referral business from
that client is always more efficient
and productive than acquiring business from
new clients in the market.

■ ■ ■

KILLING THE SALE

High trust sales professionals have a different purpose than their counterparts.

There is something bigger than the sale
that motivates them to perform their best,
and it's why every audience who takes in their
performance is compelled to applaud.
They are in the sales business for something
more than the commissions they earn
or accolades they receive. For high trust sales
professionals it's all about people.

. . .

HIGH TRUST SELLING

Your greatest competition is not out there somewhere. Your greatest competition is in the mirror. Your greatest competition is yourself. And when it comes down to it, if you can learn to continually be better than yourself—despite the mistakes you've made in the past—it won't be long before your clients will be singing your praises and clamoring for your business.

■　■　■

KILLING THE SALE

Other books by
Todd Duncan...

FROM THE AUTHOR OF THE NATIONAL BEST-SELLER HIGH TRUST SELLING

TODD DUNCAN

NO SALE

KILLING THE SALE

THE 10 FATAL MISTAKES SALESPEOPLE MAKE
AND HOW TO AVOID THEM

NEW YORK TIMES BESTSELLER

TODD DUNCAN

AUTHOR OF *HIGH TRUST SELLING*

TIME TRAPS

PROVEN STRATEGIES FOR SWAMPED PROFESSIONALS

For booking information, go to
www.toddduncan.com *or call* **866-YES-TODD**